HHB

The Long Black Veil

Poems by

Robert Cooperman

Higganum Hill Books : Higganum, Connecticut

First Edition
First Printing, September 1, 2006

Higganum Hill Books
P.O. Box 666, Higganum, CT 06441
Ph: (860) 345-4103
Email: rcdebold@mindspring.com

ISBN10: 0-9776556-1-X
ISBN13: 978-0-9776556-1-8
Library of Congress Control Number: 2006011380

Art Direction: Nancy Wynn
Designer: John Glavascich
Photography: John Glavascich
Civic Design: Tim Bayon, Emily Chionchio, David Fortier, John Glavascich, Shakeema Haynes, Matthew Hunsberger, Jessica Katz, Ron Pezzullo, Brendan Sullivan, Stephanie Trainor

---

Library of Congress Cataloging-in-Publication Data

Cooperman, Robert.
  The long black veil : poems / by Robert Cooperman. -- 1st ed.
     p. cm.
  ISBN 0-9776556-1-X (alk. paper)
  I. Title.
  PS3553.O629L66 2006
  811'.6--dc22
                                        2006011380

Independent Publishers Group distributes Higganum Hill Books:
Ph: (800) 888-4741   www.ipgbook.com
Printed in the United States of America.

Dedication

"This one, as they all are, is for Beth"

ACKNOWLEDGEMENTS

The author wishes to thank the editors of the journals listed below, where the following poems first appeared, in earlier form and with slightly altered titles:

Antietam Review: "Old Lem William"

California Quarterly: "During the Trial, Emma Ritchfield Considers Her Husband"

Coal City Review: "Hiram Wheatley, the Mine's Chief Bookkeeper, the First Witness"

Crosstimbers Magazine: "Emma Ritchfield, Below the Gallows," "Conner Ritchfield, Below the Gallows"

Hard Road To Hoe: "In Jail, Miller Waggoner Remembers the Death of Conner Ritchfield's Parents"

Louisiana Literature: "Louise Early, Miller Waggoner's Housekeeper"

Main Street Rag: "Sheriff Alvin Gallatin"

Mobius: "Tom Whitby, the Man Who Ran," "Zerelda Higgins, the Judge's Wife," "Voodoo Sally, the Judge's New Cook"

Nassau Review: "Emma Ritchfield, Dying"

Parting Gifts: "On the Gallows, Simon Purefoy, Minister," "On the Gallows, Shadrach Brown, Hangman"

Pegasus: "Emma Ritchfield Visits Miller Waggoner's Grave," "The Lady in the Long Black Veil Takes Revenge," "Emma Ritchfield, Ten Years Later," "Miller Waggoner, Ten Years After His Hanging"

The South Carolina Review: "Conner Ritchfield Sits Through the Murder Trial," "Louise Early Walks by Night"

Waterways: "Emma Ritchfield, As Her Husband Lies Dying," "Conner Ritchfield, on His Deathbed," "Emma Ritchfield, at Her Husband's Funeral"

CONTENTS

PART III—AT ETERNITY'S GATE

PART IV—SECRETS AND LIES

PART V—THE LONG BLACK VEIL

"The Long Black Veil"
(by Marijohn Wilkin and Danny Dill)

Ten years ago on a cold dark night
There was someone killed 'neath the town hall light.
There were few at the scene, and they all did agree
That the man who ran looked a lot like me.

The judge said, "Son, what is your alibi?
If you were somewhere else then you won't have to die."
I spoke not a word though it meant my life,
For I had been in the arms of my best friend's wife.

Chorus

She walks these hills in a long black veil,
She visits my grave when the night winds wail.
Nobody knows, nobody sees,
Nobody knows but me.

The scaffold high, eternity near,
She stood in the crowd, she shed not a tear.
But sometimes at night when the cold wind moans,
In a long black veil she weeps over my bones.

Chorus

She walks these hills in a long black veil,
She visits my grave when the night winds wail.
Nobody knows, nobody sees,
Nobody knows but me.

Part 1

Taken

Miller Waggoner Is Taken for Murder

Orion still drawing his bow of stars,
Sheriff Gallatin stood at my door,
as if desperate for a spittoon.
At last he apologized that he'd come
to arrest me for murdering Mr. Edwards,
our honest-as-the-day-is-long banker.

When he finally got it all out,
like a schoolboy attempting to recite
a tongue twister from Shakespeare,
I saw the hell I'd thrust myself into:
thrashing in the heaven of Emma Ritchfield
while the murder was being done.

"God has Satan's sense of humor,"
I thought, for how could I defend both
my innocence and Emma's honor?
Worse, how could I escape the gallows
and Conner's rage: betrayed by his wife
and me, his lifelong best friend?

"Make a clean breast of it,"
Gallatin sadly coaxed, a better
drinking and poker pal than priest.
"Breast," I thought, "yes, Emma's,
so soft, so white, so lost to me now."

I sit in jail, silent as the Sphinx
I always fancied visiting with Emma.
I've told my lawyer not to try too hard.

"But you're throwing your life away!"
he roared, between nips from his flask.
"Sometimes," I clapped his back,
it's the only thing to do with it,"
and slugged the moonshine he handed me.

Tom Whitby, the Man Who Ran

Mary groaned
weak as a starving pup,
while the Old Witch Woman
shook her head,
my eyes pleading for a miracle.

Mary didn't even know
me anymore — pain smudging
every sweet memory —
so I left to buy some moonshine,
and forget everything.

I strode for the Town Hall,
men always sharing
nighttime jugs on its steps;
but first I spied Banker Edwards.

My hate boiled
like stirred up yellow jackets —
he'd refused to lend us money
for a Charleston doctor
instead of the company quack,
with his drink-quaking hands.

My knife plunged into his miserly guts.

Blood running black as slag
over his fingers,
Edwards stared, not recalling
he'd swatted me from his office
like a gnat a week earlier,
saying, "Your wife will die
whatever you do,
so why waste bank assets
you'll never repay?"

"Remember me now?"
I taunted, then ran.

In Jail, Miller Waggoner Remembers the Death of Conner Ritchfield's Parents

"I don't know what I'd do without
your friendship propping me up,"
Con had raked his forehead:
his pappy and meemaw dying
in their overturned buggy,
the old man never one to ease up
on the whip when he was in a hurry.

We stood by their graves,
Conner's head bowed,
his yellow hair death-moth pale.
That night, he cried he couldn't go on.

"You got no choice," I told him,
my parents and sister long dead
but still grieved in the quiet nights.
"Too many miners and their families
depend on you," I gripped Con's arm
like General Lee slapping courage
into a private before a big battle.

Still, he left Tennison, begged me
to tend to his mine in his absence,
swore he'd make it right in the end,
but he needed some time alone,
and when he returned,
Emma was shining on his arm.

I'd have followed him into hell,
but march him into my own perdition
if he ever finds out.
The only woman I've ever loved,
and she had to be my best friend's wife.

In Jail, Miller Waggoner Remembers His First Meetings with Mrs. Emma Ritchfield

When Conner returned
from his odyssey of grief,
I met him at the depot,
on his arm an angel.
"My sparkling bride, Emma."
Her smile banished the coal dust
that glooms our hills.
I stood gape-mouthed
as mad Ike Samson.
"You'll catch flies," she laughed.

At dinner, Emma spoke
of stifling South Carolina
as if singing the old hill ballads,
"So I sought broader vistas," she trilled.
"You'll not find them here," I joked,
"hemmed in by hollers and gossip."

Over brandy, Conner remarked:
"I'm called away to Morgantown,
and since you're an idle dog,
I expect you to entertain my lily of the hills."
Emma pouted at his abandonment
so early in their marriage,
but Conner allowed only mourning
to pry itself between him and business.

Twice I called on my friend's wife,
twice we talked of Conner.
Our third outing, rain disrupted
the picnic my housekeeper prepared;
I geed up hard for my hunting cabin,
and while our clothes hearth-dried—
oh, it was sweet as licking honey.

We swore it would be the last time
we'd ever betray Conner,
but of course it was only the first.

A Townsman Comments

About time
them Waggoners
got took down:
him the last
of that stuck-up brood
no trouble ever touched,

though his sister drowned,
and his ma ended
in an asylum,
and his pappy took
his favorite imported pistol
to his head.

Still, I'll waste no pity
on a killer,
witnesses certain
as Judgment Day
his silver dagger did
for Banker Edwards.

A man like me,
who toils his life away
for coal mine owners
and strangle-handed bankers,
don't get to enjoy
too many spectacles.

So a murder trial
followed by a hanging's
something I look forward to.

In Jail, Miller Waggoner Thinks Further About Emma Ritchfield

Con told Emma of our boyhood
exploits so often, she recited them to me
like the tunes the three of us sang
when they invited me to dinner,
songs about silver daggers
protecting chaste maidens,
or lovers faithful past the grave,
Emma's and my voices catching
for an instant as if on barbed wire
meant to keep out trespassers.

It hurt to hear those childhood tales
of coming across unguarded stills
or swimming in Tillman's Pond
and hiding Floyd Digby's britches:
a heaven I've tossed away,
for the sweet hell of adulterous love.

Still, I laughed when she reminded me
of the time Conner was run up a tree
by a black bear; I saved him
by pitching rocks off its head
till it snorted and ambled off.
Except in his version,
Con saved my sorry hide.

"Is that what he told you?"
I caressed her alabaster bosoms—
whiter for her hair being black
as the song of a true love's tresses.

Miller Waggoner Ponders His Reputation with the Ladies

"Fox in the hen house,"
men called me, but I swear
ladies were always after me
because of the face I never asked for,
the tongue that flattered them:
Meemaw insisting that all men
must practice etiquette and courtesy.

With Emma I tried doubly hard
to behave, but a storm knocked us flat
the moment Conner brought her
to these hills and coal hollows.
If she'd been a flirt,
we'd have bandied words
and no harm done.
But when she stared at me,
I was the old ballad's Mattie Groves,
and she my star-crossed
fatal angel, Lord Barnard's wife.

I tried to hide how I felt,
but she sniffed it out
like a hobo drawn by a pie
three counties off.
One thing led to another,
and we were so deep into lies
and each other
there was no way out
but by digging deeper,
or pulling apart,
which would've killed us.

My hanging will make amends
for stealing her like Gypsy Davy
in the song Emma loved:
her way of saying she'd run with me
to the sooty end of the earth
that would bloom for us like flowers.

Part 2

The Weight Of Evidence

Hiram Wheatley, the Mine's Chief Bookkeeper:
the First Witness

Ever since my wife died,
I walk and drink at night,
leaving my free company cottage
to mice, dust, and spider webs.

The night Edwards was killed,
Thompson and I were passing
my flask, my eyes heavy
as Becka's curtains that threaten
to stifle me now that she's gone.

Still, it *was* Waggoner I saw:
no mistaking his mustache,
the thrust of his shoulders.

He'd tip his fancy hat to Becka,
to make her simper like a quail
after she took sick
but could still walk downtown
for some light shopping
or just to sip a phosphate.

Night after night after night
of her groaning pain drove me
to give her an extra dose of morphine,
but she didn't stop breathing.
Sobbing, I smothered her; she fought,
though I'm sure she wanted me
to end her agony.

Luther Thompson, the Second Witness

Midnight's too early to limp home
to my squawking old lady,
what with Nona's perfume reeking
like a love-still all over me.

Wheatley had him a flask,
so we set on the Town Hall steps
when we saw Banker Edwards,
though what he was doing out
that time of night I don't know.
Then we spied Miller Waggoner,
who ran, gripping a knife.

After we told the sheriff,
I strutted home a hero.
But Emily snorted,
"Civic duty! you with breath
a dragon would hide from.
I can smell floozy-syrup
under all that corn mash;
I catch you two at it,
I'll have your worm for bait.

"Now get to bed, you gotta run
the mine elevator first shift:
all you're good for after that shoring
busted up your worthless,
drunkard's leg."

Lord in Heaven,
that woman can nag louder
than overworked brakes
on a full trainload of coal—
too bad Waggoner didn't stab her.

On Trial, Miller Waggoner Thinks of Love and Music

It wasn't all just writhing
like crazed snakes in a dark hole.
We talked too, laughed,
sat in long, easy silences;
and we sang together,
from the harmony in our hearts.

I taught Emma all the old tunes:
melodies of terrible journeys
and happy homecomings,
of true loves and girls betrayed,
and men who trusted gals
who loved gold rings more.

The first time I sang to her,
I schooled her,
"These songs are who we are
up here in the coal hills,"
and picked a tune on the guitar.

"Then they're my songs too,"
Emma stroked my jaw, kissed me,
and soon our love cries rose
like wolves and cougars
in their wild ecstasies,
all gentler songs forgotten.

But looking back now
while the prosecutor parades
his witnesses, maybe we sang
not so much to share the music
swelling in our hearts,
but to drown out the guilt
shrieking in our souls.

The Testimony of Ike Samson, Village Idiot

Folks call me "Idjit Ike,"
but that night I saw Mr. Miller
with Mr. Conner's missus.

I crept up to the window:
Mr. Miller and her nekkid,
her sobbing afterwards
about them running off together.

When he was took for murder,
I snuck into court and shouted,
"He weren't even there!"

Mrs. Emma went red
as tomatoes boys throw at me,
Judge smacked his hammer
like he wished it was my head;
even Mr. Miller rose big and dark
as a full coal car without no brakes,
though his lawyer tried
to get me in the witness box.

Instead, I was tossed in jail,
Mr. Miller in the next cell.
"Whyn't you let me
tell the truth?" I cried.

"Sometimes," he sighed,
"truth hurts too damn much."

Can't hurt worse
than the rope he'll jerk from
like a worm on a hook.

Judge Mangrove Higgins, After Ike Samson's Outburst

I won't stand disruptions
in my courtroom,
especially from Ike Samson,
that drooling moonshine moron.

When Ike shouted,
"Mr. Miller wasn't even there!"
I gaveled so hard
my mallet shattered
like a buckshot-pigeon.

Waggoner was guilty all right;
why else refuse even
a perfunctory defense?
Still, I noticed how ashen
his face went
when Ike sputtered and spewed.

It made me suspect
something wasn't right.
But damnit, if a man won't
rise to his own defense
with some spirit,
that's not a judge's job.

So why does it gnaw my guts
like my last cook's leaden
pork chops, the look
Ike Samson shot me
as the sheriff and deputy
wrestled him out of my court —

that for once he knew
what I was too thick to see?

Tom Whitby, in the Courthouse During the Murder Trial

I shrink into the back wall
while Waggoner refuses
to let his lawyer speechify.
I'd've hopped a freight,
but I'm drawn to this trial
like a man staring over a cliff.

Our son had the sense
to quit this coal mining hell,
even if he's just a hobo now:
black lung picks us off up here
like a damn Federal sniper.

I doubt we'll meet again in this life.
As for the next one,
I'm going to a desert hotter
than the one he wrote us of
that one time, from Out West.

He's a mystery; so's Waggoner,
who won't allow his lawyer
to cross-examine witnesses now.

"You fool," I almost shout
at that damn Miller Waggoner,
"what you playing at?"

Mary could cipher him,
if only she had the strength
to walk to the courthouse.

Lester Freeman, Jury Foreman

Not a man in town Miller Waggoner
ain't loaned money to in hard times.
You'd think he was taking charity
when anyone tried to pay him back.
So when the judge sent his bailiff
into the jury room to nudge us along,
I told Mingus McGhee,
"We got evidence to consider."

"Evidence?" he spat tobacco on the floor.
"The man's guiltier'n Cain and Judas.
'Sides, Judge wants his dinner."

"That's not our concern,"
I shut the door, and glanced at men
sadder than a wake without moonshine.
"I guess we got to vote," I sighed.
Shocked me one read, "Not Guilty."

"That'd be me," Henry Till raised
a hand like we were still schoolboys.
"What's your proof?" I asked, hoping.
"Just the horse sense to know
Miller wouldn't kill for no reason,
and no one's showed me any."

"Henry," I rubbed my forehead,
"we got two eye-witnesses."
"Two drunks!" he shot back
like a squirrel gun.

"He offered no defense," I said.
Henry slumped in defeat; we prayed
for Miller's soul and our own,
then trudged back to the courtroom
like a chain gang.

Conner Ritchfield Sits Through the Murder Trial

"I know you couldn't
have committed this act,"
I assured Miller,
while he awaited trial.

"I was in dreadful debt," he sighed,
"and when Edwards sneered
my credit was worthless as a Yankee,
the knife just leapt into my fist."

"Why didn't you ask me for the money?"
I demanded; he shrugged apologies,
and suddenly I didn't know the man
I'd grown up with, mingled blood with
when we swore eternal friendship.
"You're protecting someone!"

"Your wife," he joked, to let me know
I'd once again followed a false trail,
like when we were boys out hunting,
and he found the pathless way back to town.

Now, I sit in court, Miller refusing
to allow his lawyer to raise objections
to lies more outrageous than any spewed
by Friday night drunken miners.

When "Guilty!" is finally delivered,
Emma faints beside me; my poor darling.

Emma Ritchfield Sits Through the Murder Trial

Every time that brute
of a prosecutor hammers
a piece of damning evidence
into his anvil palm,
I want to rise and shout,
"Miller was with me that night!"
But I remain silent and safe,
though we women forever bray
we're the equals of men for bravery.

When my husband and I visited
Miller in jail before the trial,
I asked Conner to wait outside
a moment, telling him I'd try
to reason with his best friend.

"You must tell the truth,"
I hissed when we were alone.
"My reputation's a lie!"

"Do you think anyone will believe us?"
he sighed, "aside from Conner,
and he'll hate you into the grave."
Before we could think, we kissed,
tears slashing our faces.

Now, as I sit in court,
the confession again bubbles,
for I see the jury's searching for
any excuse to hurrah Miller's innocence.
But in the instant before I rise,
Conner takes my hand; my courage
fades like the sweet stars
into the mist-bitter dawn
on that first night
Miller and I stole together.

During the Trial, Emma Ritchfield Considers Her Husband

Conner, I'd never have married you
had I known the heartache I'll cause,
when it will finally fall on you
like rotted shorings that I betrayed you
with your most trusted friend.

When you and I first met
in my suffocating South Carolina,
I thought you exotic as a Bedouin.
But home in your West Virginia
coal hills after our honeymoon,
you shape shifted from the beau
who courted me with songs, poems,
stories, and dance-floor valor
into just another pompous mine owner.

Not a week after we set up house,
you were off on business to Morgantown.
The day after you sent that telegram
stating you'd be delayed returning,
Miller—meant as my safe chaperone—
and I were caught by a storm,
and took shelter in his hunting cabin.

Though he'd chivalrously swear
he was my seducer,
one instant I was mummified
in a scratchy blanket
while my dress and petticoat dried;
the next—seething with rage at you
and passion for him—I let the blanket fall,
his breath the rushing of the tide.

We were tranced, the spell irrevocable.
But my soul shouts, "No excuse!"

Judge Mangrove Higgins Pronounces Sentence on Miller Waggoner

When I point blank demanded
where in tarnation he was that night,
his face went pale as a poison mushroom,
for he knew silence was his only chance
to win his race with the gallows.

The one time he showed gumption:
when his lawyer whispered something.
Then he flew into a catamount rage,
and when I gaveled him to shut up,
sit down, and mind his manners,
a scowl slashed his face
like the scars mine trash earn
in their drunken knife fights.

And when I pronounced sentence,
that foolish Ritchfield woman swooned:
there's always one who's glamored
by a handsome murderer.

Afterwards, I repaired home
quick as an empty coal train,
for we'd hired a new darkie cook
renowned for her Lowland cuisine,
and for dabbling in the black arts.

My wife's breath is brimstone,
her voice sharp as barbwire;
in bed she's a lust-mad banshee:
no wonder I fail
to rise to the occasion.

Zerelda Higgins, the Judge's Wife

If Miller Waggoner had cast
one smoldering glance at me,
I'd have left my husband,
Mr. Waggoner our tragic knight
for having committed a murder
every woman in town devoutly
wished he'd be acquitted for.

When my husband finally divulged
Mr. Waggoner's hard fate—
after first devouring our cook's dishes—
I ran up to my room and sobbed,
though Mr. Waggoner had never
done more than tip his hat to me,
chat amiably at dinner parties,
or compliment my performances
in our Mountain Players' Theatre.

Our cook dabbles in potions,
so laughing careless as a merry widow,
I asked if she had anything
to inspire a less than diligent consort.
She handed me a vial that smelled
of Hades' sulphur pits, and scowled,
"The best salves go bad on some men."

Our next murder trial may be mine,
after I bury a carving knife
in my husband's belly, sated
as seven dragons on our cook's cuisine:
a prophetess, I fear, at spells and salves.

Voodoo Sally, the Judge's New Cook

I didn't need no Sight
to see Miller Waggoner
no more killed that banker
than white folks'd let me
into their parlors with anything
but a serving tray and a smile
sparkling and phony as a fifth ace.
Him and his married lady friend
should've run off together that night.

I'm heading back to Savannah.
Of all the white folks I've toiled for,
Judge and his Missus the orneriest
pair of pecking buzzards,
though she begged me for a love potion,
tittering she didn't believe
in "such darkie nonsense."

I saw the hunger in her eyes,
him more interested in his belly
than pleasing a wife dying
to love him up and down.

Back in sunny Savannah
I'll open my own eatery,
get me a white silent partner
to smile for customers,
whilst I fricassee and fry,
stir up potions and remedies.

As for that Miller Waggoner,
his hanging will be a lot quicker
and more merciful than the doom
the Judge's wife got to spend
the rest of her life sentenced at.

Part 3

At Eternity's Gate

Emma Ritchfield Remembers the Night of the Murder

I had steeled myself
never to see Miller again.
But when the hour approached—
my husband once again out of town—
the house whispered, "Go to him!"

I ran to the cabin
where he and Conner fished and hunted.
Sweating in his arms, I begged Miller
to take me from this coal-rich prison.
"All right," he finally agreed.
We ran to pack and meet before dawn.

But by the time I reached home,
Conner had returned, pacing the floor,
wringing his hands like an old woman,
and saying Miller had been taken
for murder, and not a thought
about where I'd been, thank God.

"Go to the jail," I commanded,
"tell the sheriff he has the wrong man."

"I've already been," he sighed,
as if a lovesick girl in a novel,
and not the hero who'd sweet-talked
and sang me into marrying him.

The rest of that night
we clung to each other,
as if two survivors of a shipwreck.
Be it grief or guilt, I don't know,
but when he stroked and kissed me,
I gave myself to him with a ferocity
that startled the both of us.

Benton Timmons, Defense Attorney

Waggoner sat with arms folded
while my worthy opponent
paraded his few eyewitnesses:
always the most dramatic testimony,
though highly suspect that night:
no streetlamps but the one
atop the Town Hall casting its gloom.

Yet two men who'd stopped to gossip—
and share a flask—swore
my client ran, knife in hand.

Throughout the droning evidence,
it slapped me like the flat
of Justice's blind sword
that Waggoner was hiding something.
I turned, saw Emma Ritchfield,
and knew it was some married woman
without the courage to appear in court.

Gripping my client's arm, I hissed,
"Which rich slut are you protecting?
Doesn't Edwards deserve justice!"

Miller banged his fist and told me
to mind my own damn business,
which, considering where we were,
I found inordinately funny.

As soon as the verdict was delivered,
I allowed him to shake my hand—
for all the good I'd done him—
then ran to my office and pulled the cork
from the jug I keep in a desk drawer.

Ludlow Haversham, the Prosecutor

With an election imminent,
I needed a conviction, especially
since the victim was our banker,
citizens coddled that their deposits
were safe as eagles' eggs in high nests.

Miller Waggoner put up no defense,
refused to unleash Lawyer Timmons,
who regularly tosses motions,
briefs, and objections to defer justice
when it needs to be swift and sharp
as a butcher's slaughtering blade.

Was it my task to throw out the case,
even if I suspected the two witnesses
were so sauced they couldn't see
a mile of crawling coal cars at noon,
let alone a man running off
in a misty and dim midnight?

Besides, Waggoner cuts a dashing
figure the ladies can dream of.
He'll stand chest thrust out, reciting
some last verses of tragic poetry
or sing a sweetly sad hill ballad,
while he waits on the gallows.

A mistrial might cast doubts
on my competence to serve and protect
the good citizens of our fair town.

Tom Whitby at the Hanging

At the trial Waggoner sat
silent and heavy as the idiot stick
I shovel up coal with,
'stead of trying to argue himself
out of that necktie I deserve.

Now, it's clear as a trout stream
coal trains ain't dumped slag in yet,
that woman over yonder
with her husband, the lady staring
at Waggoner like he's angel food cake,
the one who swooned at his trial
when the verdict was read,
she's the one he's protecting.

I could get money out of her,
for Mary's sake: maybe not too late
for a Charleston doctor's miracle,
though she breathes shallower
than a slick of bacon grease
on moldy bread.

I need a long pull, to think straight:
too long since corn lightning
jolted me into visions
clearer than any lied about
by snake handlers bragging
how many times they've seen Jesus.

But here's Waggoner, acting
like that scaffold ain't
nothing to do with him.
I won't feel safe till after
he's took down from the gallows,
no telling what that lady
might say to get him off.

Miller Waggoner Walks to the Gallows

Kinder to all of us
had Emma and I run off
the first time
our blood and bodies
went wild in each other:
for Con will find out,
both their lives a hell
of blame and guilt.

Though I go to the gallows
silent as a buried stone,
someone must've seen us
and will tattle long and loud:
this town delighting in gossip
as if freeing flocks of doves.

Daddy warned me
the ladies'd be my ruin.
He was right
though he had a tongue
slick as a drummer
of silk unmentionables,
for vexing the tender sex,

but lucky enough
never to get enmeshed
in the chains I've forged
to drag myself under.

Emma Ritchfield, Below the Gallows

This is the moment I've dreaded
since this nightmare began,
Miller nodding for the hood.

I wish to God I were still
Conner's delirious bride,
Miller just our dear friend,
a third voice to sing with
and make up a card partner
on evenings of pleasant fellowship.

Though I swore to myself
I'd watch with a valiant heart
as my darling died for my sake,
I squeeze shut my eyes,
flinch at the trap's thunder,
the bullwhip snap of the rope.

When Conner sighed,
"I must attend the execution
for Miller's sake,"
I said, "I shall too,"
as if from married loyalty,
to earn his grateful kiss.

Lord, give me courage to beg
his forgiveness, someday.
He grips my arm, sobs for his friend.

Conner Ritchfield, Below the Gallows

I should've shouted in court,
"Waggoner was with my wife
when Edwards was killed!"
But I held my coward's peace,
afraid my brave lie
would make me a laughingstock
in this town that worships gossip.

Children would snicker,
adult fingers point like daggers
when I'd pass by alone;
or worse, Emma on my arm;
worse still, the pitying looks;
and most dreadful of all,
Miller would still be found guilty,
everyone knowing I'd do or say
anything to save him.

Ladies would wonder loudly
when Emma would again play me
like a spent trout;
men would wink and tap their noses
that there's nothing so treasured
as an honest woman.

While grapeshot-rain falls,
Miller says a sad goodbye
to me with his eyes,
then nods for the hood
as if we're still playing
our childhood game of Gallant Spy
and Treacherous Yankee,
blood brothers forever.

On the Gallows, Simon Purefoy, Minister

When I stood beside him
on the drenched scaffold,
I gently urged Mr. Waggoner,
"Confess your remorse in plain,
manly language, and ease your pain
in the World that awaits us all."

Through the soot-cold rain,
the condemned man whispered,
"I didn't kill that fat leech,"
then nodded to the hangman.
Mr. Waggoner's legs jolted,
then went still, forever.

Long after he was cut down,
I stood in the razor rain,
my black hat's brim drooping
like a desperately ridden mount,
boots filling with frozen water
as if battlefield blood,
wondering what would possess
a man to throw away his life,
his immortal soul.

Finally, shuddering,
I limped slowly home
to my own dear wife's
comforting arms
and the warm bath
she had waiting for me.

On the Gallows, Shadrach Brown, Hangman

I heard what he whispered
to the minister: about being innocent.
But when Mr. Waggoner nodded
he was ready, professional
habit took over.

I've had to drag men up here,
their knees soggy as fence posts
after a flood, men that threatened—
like Moses smashing the Tablets—
their ghosts would exact vengeance,
men swearing by their buried mothers
they were clean as washed babies,
but their meemaws were standing
under the scaffold begging them
to confess and go white to Jesus.

But I never heard one whisper
his innocence like a practical joke.
I ain't clever, just good
at measuring the condemned
for quick and painless retribution.
It set me to pondering why he'd wear
that pinching necktie in sooty sleet,
many a wretch before him muttering,
"Come on, 'fore I freeze to death."

I'll be damned if I can figure it:
leaving us with a killer cocky
about getting off, and maybe tempted
to try that fatal game a few more times.

Sheriff Alvin Gallatin

It pained me to the heart
to arrest Miller Waggoner—
a man I'd fished, hunted,
played poker, and drank with.
But we had witnesses.

When I came for Miller,
he laughed like he'd expected me,
and when the verdict was read—
to much weeping from the ladies,
the jurymen, and even me—
he stood like the sentence of death
was a decoration for battle valor.

He walked as calm
to the gallows as General Lee
surrendering at Appomattox,
the only man not shivering
from that sleet of frozen nails.

Miller was a gentleman
first to last, not wanting
to cause any more trouble
than he already had.

Up to me,
I'd never have arrested him:
innocent or guilty,
these hills are big enough
for a man to hide in
and do no further harm,
for the rest of his days.

Part 4

Secrets And Lies

Mrs. Althea Edwards, Widow of the Slain Banker

Why my hero of a late husband
was out walking at midnight,
I'll not say aloud: tongues wag
in this town like the tails of curs
that wait till your back is turned
before they snap and snarl.

But he was on his way
to rob his own bank,
then bolt like a cob stampeding
from a lady's carriage.
He wanted a fresh start
with a new Eve,
far from his wife and son.

He hated this town,
and in that, at least,
I applaud his good sense:
cliffs so steep it's black
as a mineshaft, all year long,
eternal darkness, too,
from floating coal soot
grittier than forest fire cinders.

I bless Mr. Waggoner:
making it easy for me
to inherit everything,
sell the bank, and move
where my little Freddie
can shake off the coal dust
of this grim hinterland,
thick as battlefield grime.

Frederick Edwards, Age Fourteen, Son of the Slain Banker

Meemaw thinks I'll follow her
to Richmond like a river's channel.
Shoot, I'll sneak off to live
with Old Lem Williams,
a farmer before his hands
got gnarled as pine knots.
But the stories he tells!

Pa was too tame for this coal town,
nor did he take to the woods
with its game that Lem traps.
"Nothing so good," he teaches me,
"as what you catch and kill:
next best thing to being an Injun."

'Sides, there's Ginny Appleby,
her hair bright as a fox
that's snatched a fat laying hen,
almost as good at snaring game
as Lem is, and silent as a Choctaw
pointing out a doe giving birth.

A good thing Pa's killer hanged,
or I'd have to get him:
the law in these hills and hollers
when it comes to avenging kin,
though Lem swears, against
all the witnesses and speeches,
it wasn't Mr. Waggoner.

Lem says sometimes
your eyes can be dead wrong,
but your heart, never.

Old Lem Williams

Miller Waggoner knew I poached
his daddy's land, but said nothing,
so I'll not speak against him, even if
he swung for murdering Banker Edwards.
Hell, Miller should've kilt a passel
of bankers for all I cared:

My boys died in the War,
left me with not enough hands
or strength to work my land;
and when Banker Edwards smiled
with a pile of papers for me to sign,
I trusted him and got run off:
to live on game and selling moonshine,
though I gave it to Miller,
along with tales of Injuns and catamounts.

I make up stories for Banker Edwards'
son Freddy, and tell him, too,
wasn't Miller kilt his daddy—
a lie to save a friend's reputation,
but not as big a lie as the one
General Lee's recruiters promised:
that the War would be over in weeks,
our sons home in time to sing carols
and get their jaws all greasy
on good Christmas ham.

Hell, no one's ever even seen
a darkie slave in these hills.
My boys died for rich
Lowland planters' sons
with no gumption to fight the War
they yapped for us to believe in
like it was Jesus rising
from His grave, all over again.

Thomas Mulgrew, the New Bank President

Miller Waggoner was a saint
of generosity to all in need,
unlike my murdered predecessor—
who'd wring his hands with pleasure
to call in outstanding loans
like truant boys whacked
by a principal's birch sapling.

So why, I ask myself, not above
speculating about my neighbors,
did Miller kill Mr. Edwards?

I believe bad-woman blood:
though I'd not think Mrs. Edwards
a doe-eyed lovely to inspire beaus
to rampage like autumn-rutting bucks.
Still, men have killed for homelier Helens.

But there's another possibility:
that Waggoner hanged to protect another.
But who, who? my curiosity
a balked bird of prey.

By now I'm as confused as my wife
after she sips a surreptitious bottle
of the sweet brandy
that wallops her like a rockslide—
her vengeance for my reading
bank ledgers late into the night,
now that she's given me two sons.

Emma Ritchfield Loses Her Baby

Part of me grieves
like a river gone dry,
but a coward's relief hisses
it was Miller's child.
That knowledge heaps layers
of mine-slag on my mourning,
for now that my lover's hanged,
I'd have cherished our baby.

While I lie in bed, Conner recites
poems to me and sings old songs
about suitors and false true loves.
I fear he's guessed my secret,
my life a hell of uncertainty.

I dreamt of Miller last night:
we were walking hand in hand,
and he sang me a song
I'd never heard before,
but one more beautiful
than oil paintings in galleries,
or fawns, or hawks in flight.

I woke to miserly mountain sun
for once pouring into my room,
and tottered to the window
and stared at trees burning
in their first autumn glory.

When Conner snaked his arms
around me and murmured,
"We'll try again and again,"
I sobbed in his startled embrace.

Miller Waggoner, Beyond the Grave, After His Lover Miscarries

I wish I had some soft words
for you, dear Emma: to assure you
that now Conner will never suspect
the boy or beloved daughter wasn't his.
But if we could speak, you'd accuse,
"Why didn't you take me from this place
and a husband I wasn't suited for,
and thus saved me, my baby, and yourself?"

In the silent mine shaft of death, I have
no words, only this hair-pulling futility
of watching those I loved and betrayed,
and with my dying, betrayed again;
for if I'd confessed I was with you that night,
then the man who killed Edwards
might have been brought to justice.

Even if it meant Conner's eternal hatred,
I'd at least still be alive to love you
far from this coal town that infects
not just our lungs, but everything:
with rumors, gossip, lies, and murder.

I can only grieve that I confused
a friend's feeling with true friendship;
grieve even more, that if we'd left,
the misery crushing your womb
would've been lifted in sunny Italy:
long easeful days of dandling our child,
not dirtying myself with owning that pit
where men die like smashed ants.

But here in the dark, I'm unable,
my darling, once again to take my leave.

45

Conner Ritchfield, After His Wife's Miscarriage

While Emma drowses
on laudanum, I croon,
"We'll have a house full of babies."
But something like suspicion
begins to mutter inside me.

I drive those thoughts out,
sit by Emma, read to her,
or hold her sleeping hand,
her hair spread black
and fine as Cherokee tresses.

But I can't believe
Miller killed the banker,
so I try to figure why
he'd let himself be hanged,
and can come up
with only one logical answer,
though I've no real proof,
just a rat gnawing my gut,
and Emma's stares:
far off as a desert in Asia.

But Christ, I miss him,
and though Emma made me gasp
with granting my wildest
loving dreams and desires,
I wish Miller and I
could've stayed
simple boys in the woods.

Louise Early, Miller Waggoner's Housekeeper

I followed him one night
after he barely touched my supper,
thinking of *her*, not me
or the way I kept his house neat
as the night before Easter morning.
She was already married, but greedy;
the pampered ones always are.

When I spied them in that cabin,
I could've set it afire;
instead, I stomped back to town.
In the square: a body, and two men
shouting *he'd* wielded the knife.
I said nothing, then or at trial,
jealousy scraping my skin off.

This way, he's mine forever.
So's the house; I take in boarders:
clean-fingered drummers;
under-accountants at the mine,
who sit at table in suit jackets
and their best manners.

I walk out of an evening with one,
a poor excuse for Mr. Waggoner,
who'd melt me like hot chocolate
when he smiled at my frying
his bacon crisp and lean.

I lie awake, feel *his* hands and lips
do wicked things to swoon me;
my cries once brought my pale beau,
thinking to ride to my rescue.
I told Walter it was only a dream,
then blew out the lamp again,
Miller beside me in all his manly glory.

Miller Waggoner, Beyond the Grave, Talks to His Former Housekeeper

Here in the silent dark of death
where you can't hear a word I'm saying,
I can truly confess that I never knew
you loved me, though that passion
would have carried less weight with me
than drifting hearth smoke:

For once I saw Emma,
we were fated like medieval lovers
flung into hell for their helpless sin;
or in my case, mistaken for the man
who killed Banker Edwards,
while I was, as you know, in Emma's arms.

I'm glad you refused to come forward,
for I went to the gallows to keep
the town and her husband—my best friend—
from knowing about Emma and me.

You were the plain hired woman
necessary as a skillet or cutting board.
But had you confessed your love,
I'd have fired you, wiped relieved sweat
with a handkerchief you embroidered,
then flung it away, with everything else
you made for me, that I finally see,
in my male blindness, were love gifts.

We men are oblivious wretches,
Louise, to all but the one woman
who sets our hears drumming
like a hound's ferociously happy tail:
as you, in dismissing your "pallid" suitor
of a boarder in the house I left to you,
have set your futile heart on me.

48

Part 5

The Long Black Veil

Emma Ritchfield Visits Miller Waggoner's Grave

Waiting for Conner's breathing
to smooth out in sleep
like the moon-calm surface of a pond,
I'm drawn to Miller's grave
as a doe can't resist the sweet grass
of a meadow fatal with hidden hunters.

I glance all around as I skim
like a river-tossed stone
from shadow to shadow,
my black veil rising and falling
like a ghost drifting through
November's freezing mists,
to proclaim, if only to myself,
that Miller was the true husband
of my heart, I his eternal widow.

I pull weeds from his plot,
plant flowers, clear fallen leaves,
murmur to his marble as if he'll answer,
embrace the cold, dark stone
and kiss it before I pick my way back
like a squaw from the spirit world.

But sometimes of late,
I'll sense a stalking shadow
near Miller's grave; I'll pivot, to face
that rascal, catamount, or haint:
nothing but wind beating
its cold wings in the hemlocks,
pines, and white oaks.

Miller Waggoner Watches His Lover Visit His Grave

Oh darling Emma,
this is the hardest of all to bear:
the sweet, choking shaft gas
of seeing you here at my grave,
and unable to stop your shuddering
with a kiss fierce as the mating
of catamounts, to give you some hope
for the long, barren life before you
with Conner, who must know—
by now—that we betrayed him.

In the old songs, true lovers
were united as roses and briars
twining into love knots atop
their side-by-side gravestones.
If you could only hear me, I'd sing
one of those old songs for you,
for the joy of remembering your smile
while we joined voices in songs,
then our wilder, wordless love duets.

You'd rush to embrace me now,
but would find your arms empty,
as your womb is of our dead child.
Had it survived, you'd have told
him or her about an old family friend;
so that part of me would've lived
and been loved by our child:
as our love briefly lifted us
to a stolen glimpse of heaven,
though that love twists into me now
like a Yankee bayonet—
to know you can't hear me,
and that we can never, never touch.

Tom Whitby Suffers a Loss and Makes a Discovery

No one but Preacher
stood beside me at Mary's fresh grave,
not even the Old Witch Woman,
complaining I'd not paid her;
but she didn't mercy Mary's pain.

After Preacher patted my shoulder
and sighed sympathy, I sat down.
Helped by some moonshine
I fell asleep, woke to full night,
a sickle moon shining dim and ghostly.

Trudging halfway down
from Mary's wood cross that'll topple
come the first nor-east blow,
I spied that lady from the hanging:
skulking along in a black veil,
and followed her to a lonely grave.

"I know all about you and him,"
I nodded at Waggoner's stone
bold as a highwayman in old songs.
She tossed me some coins and ran,
though the one I killed
and the one that hung on my account
hissed the Lord knows what I done.

Worse, Mary's haint says it ain't right.
I keep telling her it's to pay
for the fine stone she deserves,
though I squandered it all right away
on some jugs: a man needs comfort,
if there's no joy, in this anthracite life.

Louise Early Walks by Night

When I can't sleep,
I'll climb to his grave,
and whisper spells
to bring him back
like Meemaw taught me,
when I helped in the kitchen
where she worked all her life
as Mr. Miller's mother's cook.

After Meemaw's breath
rasped like an oven door,
I took over the cooking:
only Mr. Miller left to please.
Anything I set before him he swore,
"Better than French cuisine,"
to rouge my cheeks,
swell my breasts with pride.

Though he never said it in life,
I know he loved me:
why I spend so many nights
at his grave, sighing and singing.

Last time *she* was sobbing there,
stealing him even in death.
I watched her from the pines,
a branch suddenly in my fist,
when a feller came up.
She gasped, fluttered him
some coins, and ran.

"Got what you deserved,
you thieving witch!" I chuckled,
Miller all mine again.

From the Grave, Miller Waggoner Observes Emma Ritchfield and Tom Whitby

In life,
I'd have thrashed
this scoundrel
to protect Emma
from his drink-
trembling demands.

His whiskey breath
terrifies her,
and her sudden knowledge
he's the man who ran
after stabbing Banker Edwards.

I boil to get my hands
on his neck, to watch him kick,
sputter, and turn purple—
as I did, when I hanged.

Whitby swaggers
like a Yankee trooper
raiding a poor hilltop farmwife
of her last scrawny chickens,
her husband and sons killed
fighting for General Lee.

The helpless sight
of Emma cowering from him
is my true punishment
for the hell
of betraying my best friend.

Tom Whitby Meets Emma Ritchfield a Second Time

You're late,
in that black veil
that no more hides you
than a withered rose
could cover
the corpse stink of my wife,
a saint compared to you!

Why should she be dead
and you alive and pining
for some bones in the ground?

I should kill you,
but damnit you're prettier
than all the pictures
I've ever seen in books;
and by God, my knees
go watery just looking at you,

with your Injun hair,
your titties like small birds,
your mouth an invite
to fall in and drown in sweetness,
and them eyes big and black
as the chunks of coal
us poor folk gather
through shivering winters,

while the likes of you and him
laugh by roaring fires,
eat slabs of meat, drink punch
and sing the old songs
like you invented them.

You gave it to him
like a musk-mad polecat,
and goddamnit, I want it too.

The Lady in the Long Black Veil Takes Revenge

When he snarled
his new demands,
I shut my eyes
like a child afraid
of midnight monsters.

He shoved me to the ground,
fell on me, so distracted
with fumbling at his britches,

he didn't notice
I'd grabbed a rock
and hit him with it,
again and again and again,
in a shrieking frenzy.

He collapsed, heavy
as a fallen armoire.
Oh, it took Satan's own effort
to squirm free and bury him.

Now, worry wolfs my heart
his corpse will be discovered,
or that I didn't finish the brute,
or worst: his ghost will walk
with filthy, outstretched palms.

Conner Ritchfield Follows His Wife

One night
when she thought me asleep,
I followed Emma to Miller's grave.
Her black veil flung by the wind,
her small hands caressed his stone;
my tears bitter as sulphur run-off.

I glared so hard when she returned—
calm as a woman ignoring an insult—
that I prayed to go blind and deaf,
rather than know this torment.

"You two poisoned my life,"
I hurled my pipe—Miller's gift—
at the stone mantel.
Taunting fingers of fire pointed
at the biggest idiot in town,
for even dead, she loved Miller
more than she'd ever tolerated me.
She sighed relief now: no longer
having to lie and skulk and hide.

She stared, mute as a snake,
though if she'd whispered
one soft, pleading word,
I'd have kissed her and said
everything would be as it was,
and would've kept my promise.

The fire died, freezing rain
clattered against the gables
of the fine prison we shared.

All these years of missing Miller,
of loving her—one long, ugly lie.

Conner Ritchfield Discovers the Second Grave

Mocked by her betrayal,
I walked in all weather,
and on one miserable ramble
found it: soot-sharp rain revealing
the shallow grave she'd dug,
the ripped hem of the gown
I'd bought her, still clutched
by the dead man.
I buried the corpse deeper.

"I've seen your handiwork,"
I mocked Emma that evening.
"Another secret you've forced me
to keep, to my shame."

"Shout it to the hills then,"
she came back at me,
tired of my silent reproaches.

"He was blackmailing me,"
she screamed; I told her
to lower her voice:
gossiping neighbors' ears
cocked to hear an argument
five miles away.
"He tried . . .," her hand covered
her mouth and she shuddered
as if skeletal fingers reached for her.

How I longed to forgive her,
but was held captive by the tableau
I hatefully caressed in my head:
her and Miller rutting like goats,
laughing at me; worse, sobbing pity
for the poor dupe they couldn't bear
to betray, but did so, eagerly
time and time and time again.

Emma Ritchfield, As Her Husband Lies Dying

"I've seen Miller
on the Other Side,"
Conner rasped tonight,
after a cough rattled him
like a half-empty coal car.
"He curses your cowardice,"
a spasm lifted my husband—
like a canary's frantic wings
at the first whiff of gas—

and he was gone.

Strangely, I wept
though we'd been enemies
from the moment
he discovered me
kneeling by Miller's grave,
my wind-blown veil
like smoke signaling
a shaft fire.

Death's taunting grin
widened on Conner's thin face.
Tears poured from me,
torn between wanting
to strike him,
and knowing his truth
had hit me hard,
adrift now, without
the man I'd sworn
to love, but couldn't.

Conner Ritchfield, on His Deathbed

I wanted to tell Emma,
"Now that my life's running
out in spasms sooty
as our coal-fouled river,
I'm crushed by the unhappiness
we've heaped on each other.

"I watched Miller hang
for a murder whose cause
I should have guessed,
though feared to ferret out
what my trembling heart
already had started to sense."

For all that, I tried to beg
Emma's forgiveness,
but what fell from my lips
was that I'd glimpsed Miller
in the life beyond,
and he'd cursed her.

There's nothing in the grave
but the weaving of worms;
still, the hell-beast in my breast
howls to snatch
my trembling soul,
after that last act of lying spite.

Oh Emma, you should have left me
and lived with Miller, far away.
Then, you two, at least,
would've known some joy.

Emma Ritchfield, at Her Husband's Funeral

"Dear Conner,"
my tears painful as hail—
while the minister drones on
about dust, ashes,
and resurrection's uncertain hope—
"can we not forgive each other?"

Your answer: the silent clatter
of freezing curtains of rain.

Still, I miss you,
and our brief happiness:
our courtship laughter,
when you seemed a wild
and exotic beast, compared
to all my Lowland beaus;

the hiss of your whittling
some trinket for me;
the songs we sang
that fill my heart now
with such sweet sadness
for all those dead lovers
alive only in song.

I pray that you and Miller
clasp hands in Paradise,
tote fishing poles and a jug
of good mountain liquor,
and that you find
a trout stream to dream on.

While I conjure that fairy tale,
I tell myself you'd have forgiven me
had you only the strength to speak.

Emma Ritchfield, Ten Years later

I climb at night
to Miller's grave,
still wear my black veil.
Its fluttery spider-lace
the only fitting way
for me to see the world
when I visit him.

On my way back down,
I'll sit by Conner's stone,
run my hand along it, and ask
his forgiveness once again.
Then I'll return
to his silent house.

I'll try to read,
to play the old songs
Conner, Miller and I sang.
I'll curse my lover
for not defending himself;
curse my cowardice
for not shouting in court,

"He was with me,
and Lord, it was sweet!"

That declaration might not
have saved him,
but at least the simple truth.

I never returned to the city.
This hilly coal town holds me
like a wildwood flower,
though my heart breaks
every moment
of my weary life here.

Emma Ritchfield, Dying

Soon, they'll take my black veil,
cover my face with it,
and clothe me in my best dress
if the undertaker's wife doesn't steal it;
my face as spider-webbed as my veil,
Miller awaiting me in Hell:
our punishment, eternal recriminations.

Nailed to my last bed,
I relive our youthful twining times,
our bodies and souls singing in unison,
pleasure mounting to greater pleasure
for us poor wayfaring strangers
who became even stranger lovers.

But what, my heart tugs, of Conner?
Will Heaven inspire him to generosity,
or will he look down and laugh satisfaction
at the punishment we deserve?

Stupid to speculate: just worms and dirt.
Yet, like a child who still believes
in Christmas, I long to see them both,
their friendship and our love sealed
not in children's innocent blood oaths,
but Heaven's milk and honey.

Miller Waggoner, Ten Years After His Hanging

Even through your veil,
I can see Time's chisel strokes.
But to me you're lovely,
and young as honey bees.

Or perhaps those lines
were etched by the lie
Conner discovered that night
he followed you to my grave,
where you sang to me,
as we once did, after lovemaking,
or those times we had no need
of frantic caresses,
my forever fair
and tender maiden.

My love, we'll be together,
though it take ten thousand miles,
and a hundred thousand years.

Conner as well, the three of us
loving each other
not with bodies, but songs,
our souls soaring together,
all our weary wayfaring over:
a lamp ablaze in a cottage window.

AUTHOR

Robert Cooperman is the author of six previous poetry collections, most recently, *Petitions For Immortality* and *A Killing Fever*. *In The Colorado Gold Fever Mountains* won the Colorado Book Award for Poetry. Among his many chapbooks are *A Tale Of The Grateful Dead* and *Greatest Hits*.